FINANCIAL ERUDITION OF AFRICAN AMERICANS

PART 2

The Blueprint for Asset Building

Over a Lifetime

Steven E. LaBroi

The information contained in this book is provided for educational and informational purposes only and is not intended as legal, tax, investment, or financial advice. The strategies, examples, and concepts discussed reflect the author's experience, research, and professional perspective, but financial decisions should always be made in consultation with qualified professionals.

Neither the author nor any affiliated organizations make any representations or warranties with respect to the accuracy, completeness, or applicability of the content to any individual's specific circumstances. Past performance is not indicative of future results. All investing and financial strategies carry risk.

The reader assumes full responsibility for any actions taken based on the information provided in this book.

Table of Contents

Dedication

To my tribe, community, family, and friends.
Take this blueprint and share it with your family and friends.

Steven E. LaBroi

Acknowledgment

This book did not begin with me.

It began with the sacrifices, faith, and perseverance of those who camebefore me — men and women who labored, believed, and endured through systems not designed for their success. I stand on the shoulders of ancestors whose names I may never know, yet whose strength, resilience,and hope made this work possible. Their lives form the unseen foundation upon which every page of this book rests.

First and foremost, I acknowledge God — the ultimate source of wisdom,order, and purpose. Without divine guidance, knowledge lacks direction and strategy lacks meaning. The principles of stewardship, discipline, multiplication, and legacy reflected throughout this book are rooted internal truths established long before modern financial systems existed.

I offer my deepest gratitude to my family — past, present, and future. In particular, I honor my grandfathers, Duel Coffey Sr. and Lester LaBroi Sr., whose lives, values, and examples continue to shape my understanding of responsibility, integrity, and legacy.

Though they may not have used the language of financial systems, their commitment to faith, family, and perseverance planted seeds that this book now seeks to cultivate for four to five generations to come.

To my parents, relatives, and extended family: thank you for your prayers, your patience, and your belief. This work is part of our family's story, and I pray it becomes a generational blessing — one that strengthens not only our lineage, but many others as well.

I am profoundly grateful for the mentors, educators, and thought leaders who challenged me to think beyond income and toward systems. Those who introduced me to ownership, leverage, structure, and long-term vision expanded my understanding and sharpened my calling. Your influence iswoven throughout these pages.

To my colleagues — especially JD Shields—along with my clients and mentees: thank you for trusting me with your questions, your journeys, and your aspirations. Every conversation, every breakthrough, and every moment of clarity reinforced the urgency of this message. You reminded me that education changes lives—and that structure sustains progress across four to five generations.

I also acknowledge the institutions and communities that shaped me, especially Morehouse College, which instilled in me a commitment to excellence, leadership, and service.

The lessons learned there continue to inform both my professional practice and my responsibility to uplift others.

This book is written in alignment with a broader calling — Balance Life: Health, Wealth, and Faith — the belief that true prosperity is not isolated to finances alone, but is achieved when stewardship, purpose, discipline, and faith work together in harmony.

Wealth without balance is fragile; wealth anchored in values can endure for four to five generations — the equivalent of a 100-year legacy.

To the reader: by engaging with this book, you have already taken a meaningful step toward becoming a generational wealth builder —someone willing to learn from the past, act with intention in the present, and design a future that reaches four to five generations forward.

I hope that these pages challenge you, equip you, and inspire you to build financial systems that honor where we have come from and protect where we are going.

Build boldly, steward wisely, teach faithfully, and pass forward alegacy that ensures the next four to five generations — a full century of impact — begin where you left off, stronger, wiser, and prepared to carry the vision forward.

Steven E. LaBroi

Intoduction

Financial erudition is more than financial literacy — it is the disciplined, generational understanding of how wealth works, how assets grow, and how families evolve financially over time. This book is designed to illuminate the strategies, structures, and mindsets that have shaped wealth for centuries, while providing a blueprint tailored to the unique history and opportunities of African American families.

Our community has always possessed ingenuity, resilience, and brilliance. What has often been missing is access — access to systems, tools, and frameworks that convert effort into legacy. This book bridges that gap by revealing the principles that sustain wealth across decades and generations.

As you read, you'll discover how to build a foundation of assets, protect your financial life with intention, and create structures that allow your family to thrive long after your lifetime. Whether you're beginning your financial journey or refining your strategy, this guide equips you with the clarity, confidence, and courage to build a legacy that lasts.

CHAPTER 1

Legacy Change: Is It YOU?

Legacy change begins long before wealth shows up in your bank account. It begins with a decision — a moment of clarity when you recognize that your family's financial story can no longer repeat the same patterns of survival, scarcity, or missed opportunity. Legacy change starts with awareness, with ownership of your role, and with the courage to rewrite the narrative.

This chapter is written for the individual who knows, deep down, that they are the chosen one in their family — the cycle breaker, the architect, the one who steps forward to build what has never been built before. Legacy isn't simply the money you leave behind; it is the knowledge, discipline, and example you set every day. Legacy is education in action.

You may already sense this calling. You may find yourself reflecting on questions that others rarely consider:

- What is the true financial history of my family?
- How are we operating right now — not emotionally, but financially?
- What future awaits us if nothing changes?
- Why do other families seem to build wealth more easily?
- What do I keep noticing on social media, at reunions, or in conversations that tells me there is another way?

These questions are not random — they are signals. They reveal your hunger for change and your readiness to craft a different future for yourself and those who come after you.

All you need is a blueprint — a clear, practical plan that guides your next steps and gives your family something to build on for generations. The moment you choose to embrace that blueprint, everything shifts.

You are ready. Let's go deeper into the process of becoming the legacy changer your family has been waiting for.

CHAPTER 2

Accumulation Phases of Assets

The accumulation phase begins the moment something awakens inside you — a spark, an idea, an experience that opens your eyes to what's possible.

For some, it happens during a conversation with a mentor. For others, it's a book, a business opportunity, a financial setback, or even a vacation where they witness a different lifestyle and see a new standard.
Whatever the catalyst, that moment marks the beginning of intentional wealth building.

Accumulation is not about luck. It's about mindset, clarity, and structure. It starts in the mind long before it shows up in your finances. Today's world gives you more access than any previous generation — information, mentors, books, AI, and financial tools are all within reach. But access without focus becomes noise. Focus is what turns possibility into progress.

Accumulating assets begins with understanding your destination. Just like a GPS requires you to enter your end point before it can guide you, your wealth journey requires a clear vision. Once you know where you are going, the strategy becomes easier to design.

Every family's story begins in a different place. Some start from modest means. Others begin with support, exposure, or advantages that previous generations created. Regardless of your starting point, the accumulation phase gives you the power to shape a future far greater than your past.

Accumulation is not just saving money — it is building a structured, diversified portfolio of assets that grow, protect, and multiply over time. When done intentionally, accumulation becomes the foundation of your family's long-term prosperity.

This is your moment to choose intention. To stop regretting what you didn't know and begin building with what you now understand. If you can develop the blueprint, commit to it, and stay disciplined, you can accumulate the assets needed to secure the next four to five generations of your family.

Let's move forward and strengthen your foundation.

CHAPTER 3

THE FINANCIAL ERUDITION OF AFRICAN AMERICANS

Asset Accumulation

Asset accumulation is the intentional act of building wealth step-by-step, year-by-year, with clarity and purpose. It is the point where mindset becomes action and discipline becomes progress. This phase is powerful because it shifts your focus from income — which pays for your present — to assets, which secure your future.

Income keeps the lights on. Assets keep the legacy alive.
Assets are anything of value that can grow, compound, appreciate, or pay you over time. These include real estate, life insurance with cash value, business ownership, equities, precious metals, digital assets, and more.

Unlike income, assets expand without requiring your daily labor, and unlike liabilities, they strengthen your financial position rather than drain it.

When you commit to accumulating assets, you are building a fortress around your family. Assets protect you from inflation, taxes, economic downturns, emergencies, and even career transitions. They give you leverage, choices, and control.

The formula is simple but transformative:
Assets – Liabilities = Net Worth.
Your mission is to increase assets, reduce unnecessary liabilities, and grow your net worth with intention.

Think of asset accumulation as building your family's financial engine — once strong enough, it drives itself. Every property, contract, business interest, or investment you acquire becomes another cog in that engine.

One powerful example is the couple who set out to acquire 100 homes. Their goal wasn't extravagance — it was leverage. Each property became a revenue stream, an appreciating asset, and a generational shield. Their decision to accumulate assets systematically, decade after decade, created a financial foundation strong enough for generations.

Start your own journey with the same intention. Track every asset. Celebrate every acquisition. Understand that every strategic move, no matter how small, is a brick in the structure of your legacy.

Wealth leaves clues — and asset accumulation is the first major clue.

CHAPTER 4

Distribution Phases of Wealth

The distribution phase is where wealth shifts from being something you build to something you direct with purpose. This is the stage where strategy matters just as much as accumulation. Distribution is not simply about spending — it is about transferring, protecting, and positioning wealth so it serves you and future generations with precision.

As you move through life, the decisions you make around distribution determine whether your wealth lasts a lifetime... or a generation... or forever. This phase marks the transition from active wealth building to living from the systems you've created.

Some individuals accumulate wealth for lifestyle. Others accumulate it to protect their families. But the most powerful reason — the reason this book champions — is generational impact. Wealth that outlives you. Wealth that serves your children, grandchildren, and great-grandchildren. Wealth that changes the direction of your family tree.

Distribution is also where education becomes essential. You're not only passing assets — you are passing knowledge, expectations, principles, and a blueprint your family can follow. You are transferring wisdom, not just wealth.

To master distribution, you must put legal structures in place that protect your intentions. Trusts, wills, estate plans, foundations, and family offices exist to ensure your wealth does not get lost in taxes, mismanagement, or court battles. These tools preserve order, reduce conflict, and keep your financial vision intact long after you are gone.

Distribution is legacy in motion. It is the moment where everything you've built becomes the blueprint for the next generation.

CHAPTER 5

The Only Equation You Need (Assets – Liabilities = Net Worth)

The most powerful formula in personal finance is also the simplest: **Assets – Liabilities = Net Worth**. Yet despite its simplicity, it remains one of the most misunderstood and underutilized tools in wealth building.

Most people chase income; few track their net worth. But income is temporary—net worth is legacy.

This equation reveals the truth about your financial health. It shows how effectively you are building and protecting your wealth. It removes emotion and replaces it with clarity. No matter your age, income, or background, this single formula becomes your compass.

Understanding the Components

- **Assets** are anything you own that has value and the potential to grow. Real estate, cash value life insurance, retirement accounts, equities, cryptocurrency, intellectual property — these are your wealth builders.

- **Liabilities** are the obligations, debts, and consumable items that drain your resources. Mortgages, credit cards, car loans, personal loans, and lifestyle expenses reduce your net worth when they outweigh your assets.

The power of this formula is not in the math — it's in the mindset. It teaches you to think differently about money. It shifts your focus toward ownership, growth, leverage, and long-term planning.

Why Assets Must Lead

Assets create freedom. They generate income, increase in value, protect you during economic shifts, and provide collateral for greater opportunities. They move your family forward.

Liabilities, on the other hand, must be managed intentionally. When liabilities exceed assets, you enter negative net worth — a cycle that can trap families for generations.

The Formula as a Way of Life

Once you internalize this equation, every financial decision becomes intentional:

- Will this increase my assets?
- Will this add unnecessary liability?
- How does this affect my net worth over time?
- The cliché "it's not what you make, it's what you keep" becomes a guiding truth. And even beyond what you keep, it becomes about what you multiply.

Your Mission

- Memorize this formula. Teach it. Live it.
- Your goal is simple: grow assets, reduce liabilities, and build a net worth strong enough to anchor multiple generations.
- This is the equation that changes everything — the one your family will rely on long after you're gone.

CHAPTER 6

Go Deeper on Assets: Definitions and Their Importance

Assets are more than items of value — they are the building blocks of wealth, security, and generational strategy. An asset gives you stability today and leverage for tomorrow. It increases your options, strengthens your net worth, and becomes part of the financial blueprint your family will inherit.

An asset is anything you own that holds or grows in value, can produce income, or can be converted into cash when needed. These include financial assets, physical assets, contractual assets, intellectual property, and even skills.

Why Assets Matter

Assets are the backbone of long-term financial strength. They create stability, generate income, and position you for opportunities. With assets, you gain:

- Passive income that supports your lifestyle
- Collateral for borrowing and accelerating wealth
- Protection during economic uncertainty
- Liquidity for emergencies
- Transferable value for the next generation

The earlier you begin building assets — and the more consistently you accumulate them — the more powerful your financial position becomes.

Sacrificing Now for Ownership Later

Too many people exchange long-term financial security for short-term gratification. Buying liabilities with credit destroys momentum. Buying assets with intention creates legacy.

Every time you choose to invest instead of consume, you reinforce a generational pattern of financial strength. Your future self — and your future family — will thank you.

Paying Yourself First

Your income is a tool. Direct it toward ownership, not lifestyle inflation. Prioritize assets that grow and compound. Build foundational guarantees through structured products like life insurance and real estate — assets that can withstand market cycles, legislation changes, and economic volatility.

Income can fluctuate. Assets endure.

Strategic accumulation protects you not just from today's uncertainties but from tomorrow's unknowns. The world is constantly changing—technology, politics, global markets, and even the currency systems we use. Amid all that change, assets become your anchor.

Building your asset base with discipline, faith, and foresight is one of the greatest gifts you can give to your family.

CHAPTER 7

Buy Assets Every Decade: Pay Yourself First

Paying yourself first is one of the most enduring principles in wealth building. But in this blueprint, we extend that principle: you must buy assets in every decade of your life. This creates rhythm, structure, and intentionality — ensuring you grow financially regardless of age or career stage.

This strategy turns time into your greatest ally. Every decade becomes a chapter in your family's wealth story, with clear priorities and momentum built into your lifestyle.

The Power of Buying Assets Across Decades

Buying assets consistently trains your mind to think long-term. It develops discipline. It keeps you focused when others are distracted by lifestyle, pressure, or temporary setbacks. Over the course of your life, this simple practice can create a portfolio strong enough to support four or five generations.

Below is the blueprint — decade by decade.

- **Teens (10s): Build the Foundation Early**

The strongest foundations are laid early. A high cash value life insurance policy for a child or teenager creates lifetime leverage and tax-free growth. It becomes an anchor asset before they even begin working.

In today's world, teens are also building businesses online — gaming, social media, e-commerce. This is the perfect environment for family entrepreneurship. Parents and grandparents supply wisdom; children supply tech fluency and energy.

This creates a multigenerational business model that strengthens finances and relationships at the same time.

- **Twenties (20s): Learn, Earn, and Position Yourself**

Your twenties are for building skills, gaining experience, and studying the assets you want to master. Income may not be high yet, but your ability to learn is at its peak.

This is a decade of:

- Living below your means
- Building liquidity
- Minimizing liabilities
- Studying real estate, credit, business, and investing
- Leveraging early life insurance for opportunities

Your twenties should not be about perfection — they should be about positioning.

- **Thirties (30s): Focus, Grow, and Expand**

By your thirties, life responsibilities grow — career, family, relationships, and lifestyle. But this decade can also be your
wealth accelerator.

You will:

- Strengthen your income
- Join masterminds and conferences
- Continue learning your investment interests
- Buy real estate or partner with others
- Build emergency funds and retirement accounts
- Cultivate a supportive network of asset-minded peers

This decade is about building powerful habits and avoiding lifestyle traps.

Remember: **your assets should pay for your lifestyle — not your paycheck.**

- **Forties (40s): Double Down on What Works**

Your forties are about refinement and strategic expansion. You're wiser, more experienced, and more financially stable.

This is the decade to:

- Reinvest profits from earlier ventures
- Diversify risk across multiple asset types
- Strengthen life insurance portfolios
- Acquire rental properties or specialty assets (art, memorabilia, precious metals)
- Avoid overborrowing for lifestyle purchases

Your forties shape the quality of your senior years. Build smart now to enjoy peace later.

- **Fifties (50s): Maximize and Multiply**

Your fifties are about maximizing everything you've learned. Market downturns become opportunities; market upturns become leverage points.

In this decade:

- Buy more real estate
- Seek cash-flowing businesses
- Attend auctions and explore asset niches
- Borrow against existing assets strategically
- Use matured life insurance cash values for expansion

This is the decade to multiply net worth aggressively — with wisdom.

- **Sixties (60s): Protect and Prepare**

Your sixties are about consolidation, protection, and preparation for retirement.

You will:

- Shift portfolios toward lower-risk assets
- Maximize guaranteed returns
- Review Social Security and Medicare benefits
- Strengthen estate documents
- Reduce liabilities
- Ensure your real estate has strong equity

This is the moment to prepare for the "landing" of your financial plane.

Take vacations. Gather your family. Celebrate the journey.

- **Seventies (70s): Operate on Autopilot**

Your seventies are the payoff years — the time to live from what you've built.

Your responsibilities include:

- Managing distributions wisely

- Donating strategically (especially through PMAs)
- Reviewing trusts, wills, and long-term care plans
- Directing your family through succession planning
- Keeping your financial team aligned

Your vision is now your family's blueprint.

- **Eighties (80s): Teach, Train, and Transfer Wisdom**

Your eighties are about imparting wisdom. These are the years when your legacy becomes real in the lives of your heirs.

Focus on:

- Intentional mentorship
- Family traditions and rituals
- Teaching asset management and business principles
- Preparing successors emotionally and financially
- Celebrating the fruits of decades of discipline

These are your master-teacher years.

- **Nineties (90s): Rest, Receive, and Rejoice**

Your nineties are about rest and reflection — watching it brick by brick.

Buying assets every decade isn't just a strategy—it's a lifestyle. A rhythm. A covenant with yourself and your family.

This is how legacies are built. This is how families rise. This is how generations are changed forever.

CHAPTER 8

THE FINANCIAL ERUDITION OF AFRICAN AMERICANS

List of Asset Classes to Buy

Building long-term wealth requires understanding the full landscape of asset classes available to you. Wealthy families don't rely on one asset — they build diversified, strategic portfolios that protect them in all economic environments. Each asset class serves a unique purpose and plays a different role in your family's financial blueprint.

This chapter provides a clear, organized catalog of assets to consider as you build your portfolio. You may choose to specialize in one or two, but you should be familiar with all of them. Awareness expands possibility — and possibility expands legacy.

1. Real Estate – The Most Visible Asset Class

Real estate has been a cornerstone of wealth for centuries. It provides cash flow, appreciation, leverage, and tax advantages.

- Residential rental properties
- Commercial real estate
- Industrial property
- REITs (Real Estate Investment Trusts)
- Land development and raw land
- Digital real estate

Real estate remains one of the strongest wealth-building tools because it can pay you monthly and appreciate over time.

2. Equities (Stocks) – Ownership in Businesses

Stocks allow you to own pieces of companies and participate in their growth.

- Individual stocks
- Dividend-paying stocks
- Mutual funds and index funds
- ETFs (Exchange-Traded Funds)

Equities give you liquidity, growth potential, and long-term compounding.

3. Bonds and Fixed-Income Securities – Stability and Predictability

Bonds provide consistent, lower-risk returns.

- Treasury bonds
- Municipal bonds
- Corporate bonds
- Bond mutual funds

These assets are essential for risk management and long-term balance.

4. Life Insurance (Cash-Value Based) – The Foundational Contract

Life insurance is one of the most overlooked but powerful asset classes, offering tax advantages, stability, and multi-generational leverage.

- Whole Life Insurance
- Indexed Universal Life (IUL)
- Variable Universal Life (VUL)

- Guaranteed Universal Life (GUL)
- Participating Life Insurance
- Life Settlements
- Long-Term Care options

Life insurance is both a protection tool and a financial engine.

5. Precious Metals and Commodities – Tangible Value

These assets serve as hedges against inflation and economic uncertainty.

- Gold and silver
- Oil and gas investments
- Agricultural commodities

These assets preserve value when markets shift.

6. Private Equity and Business Ownership – High-Impact Wealth

Owning or investing in businesses accelerates wealth dramatically.

- Startups and entrepreneurial ventures
- Angel investing
- Franchise ownership
- Equity partnerships

Business ownership is one of the fastest paths to generational wealth.

7. Retirement Accounts – Long-Term Security

These accounts offer tax advantages for building future wealth.

- IRAs and Roth IRAs
- 401(k), 403(b), TSP accounts

- SEP IRAs and Solo 401(k)s for business owners

Tax-advantaged growth is a core wealth strategy.

8. Cryptocurrencies and Digital Assets – The New Frontier

Digital assets represent emerging opportunities as the world transitions to digital commerce.

- Bitcoin, Ethereum, and altcoins
- Decentralized finance (DeFi)
- NFTs and tokenized real estate

These assets offer high upside with high volatility — requiring education and strategy

9. Collectibles and Alternative Assets – Niche Wealth Builders

These assets can appreciate significantly when chosen wisely.

- Fine art
- Rare coins and stamps
- Luxury watches and exotic cars
- Memorabilia
- Royalties (books, music, film)

Alternative assets can create unique value and diversification.

10. Education and Intellectual Capital – The Assets Within You

Your knowledge and skills are among your most valuable assets.

- Degrees and certifications

- Courses, books, and specialized training
- Intellectual property

Skills produce income. Intellectual property produces legacy.

11. Business Structures for Tax, Growth, and Protection – Strategic Ownership

These legal frameworks provide control, protection, and tax advantages.

- LLC, S-Corp, C-Corp
- 501(c)(3) nonprofit status
- 508(c)(1)(A) Private Membership Associations
- Trusts (Revocable & Irrevocable)
- 643B Spendthrift Trusts

Business structures determine how your wealth is taxed, protected, and transferred.

CHAPTER 9

Deep Dive into Life Insurance Contracts (The Foundational Asset)

Life insurance remains one of the most misunderstood yet most powerful financial tools available — especially for families seeking long-term stability, protection, and generational wealth. When properly understood and strategically designed, permanent life insurance becomes more than a policy; it becomes a financial engine, a risk management tool, and a cornerstone asset.

For generations, African Americans were excluded from the deeper benefits of life insurance, often offered only limited policies or restricted from full participation in wealth-building products. Today, the playing field has shifted — but the knowledge has not always been passed down. This chapter restores that knowledge.

Understanding the Misconceptions

Many people still see life insurance as only a death benefit. Historically, this misunderstanding was reinforced by limited access, predatory practices, and redlining, both in real estate and insurance. African American families were often sold small burial policies or denied larger contracts designed to build wealth.

But the true power of life insurance — the living benefits, cash value growth, leverage, and tax advantages — has always been available to those who understood how to use it.

Term vs. Permanent Insurance

- **Term Life Insurance** provides coverage for a specific period. It is affordable and useful for income protection, debts, and family obligations. However, it has no cash value, expires if you outlive the term, and offers no asset-building potential.

Most people outlive their term policy, meaning the family receives no benefit. And when the policy expires, replacing it can be expensive or impossible due to health or age. Term has its place — but it is not an asset.

- **Permanent Life Insurance** (Whole Life, Universal Life, Indexed Universal Life, and others) provides lifetime coverage and builds tax-advantaged cash value. This cash value is the asset — protected by IRS Code 7702, growing tax-deferred, and accessible tax-free through policy loans.

When properly designed, permanent insurance becomes:

- A private bank system
- A collateral tool for buying more assets
- A stabilizer during economic downturns
- A legacy vehicle for multi-generational transfer
- A source of long-term liquidity

Why Permanent Insurance Is a Game-Changer

Permanent life insurance offers features you cannot get anywhere else:

- **Tax-free access** to cash value
- **Guaranteed growth** (varies by product)
- **Protection from market volatility**
- **Asset leverage** without liquidation
- **Probate-free wealth transfer**
- **Legal protections under contract law**

You can use this cash value to fund business ventures, buy real estate, consolidate debt, or seize opportunities — all without interrupting compound growth.

Riders and Customization

Modern life insurance allows for tailored optimization. Riders enhance flexibility and protection:

- Living benefits (chronic, critical, terminal illness)
- Long-term care riders
- Waiver of premium
- Child riders
- Return of premium options
- Accelerated death benefits

Riders can create additional layers of value depending on your goals and health. Always review the details — riders vary in cost and duration.

Designing the Right Policy

Policy design is everything. A poorly structured policy can be expensive and ineffective. A properly designed policy becomes a lifelong asset.

Work with an advisor who understands how to:

- Maximize cash value
- Minimize unnecessary costs
- Structure death benefits to support growth
- Integrate policies with your broader asset blueprint

Your policy should support your goals — not simply generate a commission for the agent.

Summary

Permanent life insurance is not just a financial product. It is a foundational asset — one that provides safety, growth, leverage, and legacy all within a single contract.

When understood and used correctly, life insurance becomes the bedrock of a generational wealth strategy.

CHAPTER 10

How to Leverage Your Assets and Make Them Pay for Your Life

One of the greatest secrets of wealth-building is this: wealthy people rarely spend their own money. They leverage their assets. They borrow against what they own so the asset continues to grow while the borrowed funds fuel new investments, new opportunities, or lifestyle needs.

Leverage, when done strategically, is not risk — it is acceleration.

This chapter breaks down how to use your existing assets to create more assets, how to avoid the pitfalls of poor leveraging, and how to transform your portfolio into a self-sustaining financial ecosystem.

1. Life Insurance Loans – Your Private Banking System

A properly structured permanent life insurance policy becomes one of the most powerful leverage tools available. Through tax-free policy loans, you can:

- Buy real estate
- Fund business opportunities
- Consolidate debt
- Cover emergencies
- Invest in high-return ventures

All without interrupting the compounding growth of your cash value.

Even term policies have leverage possibilities when structured with conversion options — allowing you to turn temporary coverage into a lifelong asset when the time is right.

2. Real Estate Equity – Turning Property into Power

Real estate provides one of the easiest and most common forms of leverage through:

- HELOCs (Home Equity Lines of Credit)
- Cash-out refinances
- Property-based business loans

You can use equity to purchase additional properties, diversify your portfolio, or capitalize on opportunities. Your personal financial statement (PFS) becomes a powerful tool in this phase, proving your net worth and helping you acquire larger assets.

3. Asset-Based Lending – Leverage Without Liquidation

Banks, private lenders, and brokerage firms offer lines of credit based on the value of:

- Investment portfolios
- Precious metals
- Cryptocurrency
- Art or collectibles

With these tools, you don't sell the asset — you borrow against it. But this requires discipline. Poor choices or volatile markets can create margin calls, forcing repayment.

This is why diversification is critical — one asset protects another.

4. Business Leverage – Turning Your Enterprise Into an Engine

Your business is one of your greatest assets. Its revenue, credit capability, and intellectual property can be leveraged to:

- Attract investors
- Secure lines of credit
- Expand operations
- Multiply income streams

The stronger your business financials, the more options you have. And in the era of AI and technology, well-positioned businesses can scale faster than ever before.

5. Commodities – Leveraging Tangible Assets

Certain commodities offer unique leverage opportunities:

- Gold and silver
- Artwork
- Sports memorabilia
- Luxury jewelry
- Rare collectibles

These items have markets, lenders, and established resale systems. They can be used as collateral or sold during strategic economic windows.

Even sneakers have become a leveraged market — proof that value exists wherever buyers and sellers create a demand cycle.

6. Rinse and Repeat With Intention

Leverage is not meant for consumption — it is meant for expansion. Use borrowed capital to acquire assets, not liabilities.

Let your **income** build your **assets.** Let your assets fund your **lifestyle.** Let your **lifestyle** never interrupt your **net worth.**

When you master leverage, your portfolio begins to grow on autopilot. You operate the same way wealthy families have for centuries: by borrowing strategically, compounding consistently, and multiplying deliberately.

This is the key to living free — and building a legacy that outlives you.

CHAPTER 11

Mastering Liquidity & Leverage: The Engine of Generational Wealth

Liquidity and leverage form the invisible infrastructure of every long-lasting financial dynasty. Assets create wealth — but liquidity and leverage determine how fast that wealth grows, how securely it is protected, and how effectively it transfers to the next generation.

This combined chapter unifies the concepts previously split between Chapters 11 and 12. Now, instead of viewing liquidity and leverage separately, you will understand them as a single, powerful system — a system that gives your family financial mobility, security, and multigenerational strength.

The Three Levels of Liquidity: Your Financial Command System

Liquidity exists in strategic tiers. Each tier determines how quickly capital can move and how much power you have in any economic environment.

Level 1: Immediate Liquidity (24–72 Hours)

These assets are your first response — your financial shield.

Examples:

- Checking/savings accounts
- Cash on hand
- Money market accounts

- Instant-access brokerage funds
- High cash value life insurance (same-day/next-day loan access)
- Digital payment platforms

Purpose: Emergencies, short-term needs, quick opportunities.
Goal: Maintain 6–12 months of essential expenses.
Why It Matters: Immediate liquidity prevents panic. It allows you to act instead of react and ensures you never liquidate generational assets to solve short-term issues.

Level 2: Mid-Term Liquidity (2–12 Weeks)
This is your opportunity capital — slower to access, but more powerful when activated.
Examples:

- Brokerage accounts (ETFs, mutual funds)
- Roth IRA contributions (not earnings)
- Gold and silver
- HELOCs and equity lines
- Structured notes
- Real estate equity with strong comps

Purpose: Expansion, repositioning, investment timing, major purchases.
Why It Matters: Mid-term liquidity gives you leverage during economic swings. This is where you move when everyone else hesitates.

Level 3: Long-Term Liquidity (Generational Capital)
This tier is rarely touched by you — because it is designed for your heirs.

Examples:

- Rental real estate
- Retirement accounts (401k, IRA, pensions)
- Business equity
- Annuities
- Trust-held assets
- Life insurance death benefits

Purpose: Legacy income, generational transfers, long-term security.
Why It Matters: These assets anchor the family through generations. They must be handled with structure — never liquidated emotionally.

LEVERAGING LIQUIDITY: The Wealth Acceleration Blueprint
Liquidity alone is not enough. Leveraged liquidity is what separates wealthy families from everyone else. When you learn to activate liquidity without dismantling your assets, you create the financial ecosystem that builds itself.

Below are the five pillars of leveraging liquidity.
1. Borrow Against Appreciating Assets — Never Sell Them
Wealthy families rarely liquidate assets — they borrow against them.

You should borrow against:

- Real estate equity
- Life insurance cash value
- Brokerage portfolios
- Business equity

Why? Because the asset continues to grow while you use the borrowed funds to acquire more assets.

This is how dynasties are built.

2. Use Liquidity to Seize Opportunity, Not Fund Lifestyle

Liquidity is not for:

- Clothes
- Vacations
- Cars
- Entertainment

Liquidity is for:

- Down payments
- Acquiring businesses
- Buying land
- Expanding real estate
- Strategic investments

Your lifestyle is funded by assets — not liquidity.

3. Combine Liquidity Sources to Increase Buying Power

Imagine this scenario:

- Life insurance loan → down payment
- HELOC → renovation or expansion
- Brokerage line → reserves or interest-only payments

This stacked leverage gives you the power to control larger assets with less personal cash.
This is what wealthy families do routinely.

4. Use Liquidity Tiers as Risk Management

Every liquidity tier protects the tier below it.

- Immediate liquidity protects mid-term assets.
- Mid-term liquidity protects long-term assets.
- Long-term assets protect generational stability.

This creates a financial domino effect where no single emergency can disrupt your system.

5. Teach Your Family the Liquidity Formula

Generational wealth collapses when heirs do not understand liquidity.

Your family must know:

- What assets can be accessed
- What assets should be borrowed against
- What assets should never be sold
- Who controls what accounts
- The rules for accessing trust assets
- How to use liquidity without destroying legacy

This requires training, documentation, and repetition.

Integrated Liquidity + Leverage Framework

Below is your unified model — the one your heirs can follow:

1. **Keep 6–12 months in Immediate Liquidity.**
2. **Use Mid-Term Liquidity for wealth expansion.**
3. **Protect Long-Term Liquidity at all costs.**
4. **Leverage appreciating assets — do not sell them.**
5. **Use liquidity to buy assets, not liabilities.**
6. **Teach liquidity strategy annually at your family meeting.**

This is your family's financial operating system.

Conclusion of the Integrated Chapter

When you master liquidity and leverage together, you unlock the financial freedom that wealthy families live by — and the financial discipline that keeps them powerful for generations.

Liquidity is stability.
Leverage is acceleration.
Together, they form the engine of dynasty.

CHAPTER 12

Net Worth That Lasts Four to Five Generations: The Architecture of Generational Wealth

Generational wealth is not built by accident — it is engineered. It is intentionally designed, strategically protected, and deliberately transferred. When done correctly, your net worth becomes more than a financial measurement; it becomes a multigenerational inheritance system that can support your lineage for 100 years or more.

True generational wealth is not just about assets. It is about structure, culture, education, and governance. Families who maintain wealth across four to five generations understand that wealth must be treated like an institution — not a bank account.

This chapter shows you how to create a generational wealth architecture strong enough to outlive you, your children, and your grandchildren.

The 100-Year Legacy Blueprint

To build wealth that spans a century, you must think like a dynasty. This means creating:

1. A Family Strategy (Your Mission & Vision)

Wealthy families operate with shared purpose. This includes:

- A family mission statement
- Generational goals
- Clear values and expectations
- Defined roles for family members

Without unity, wealth fragments. With purpose, wealth compounds.

2. A Structure of Ownership (Your Organizational Blueprint)

Generational wealth requires legal and financial structures that outlive individuals.

These structures include:

- Revocable and irrevocable trusts
- 508(c)(1)(A) Private Membership Associations
- Family foundations
- LLCs and holding companies
- 643B Spendthrift trusts

These tools provide protection, tax efficiency, and continuity.

3. A Communication System (Your Family Governance Plan)

Communication is the glue that holds wealth together.

Every generational family needs:

- Annual legacy meetings
- Financial education for each generation

- Documentation of processes and decisions
- Clear succession plans

Your heirs must know what they are inheriting and how they are expected to manage it.

The Family Office Model: How Dynasties Stay Organized

A Family Office is the command center for generational wealth. While the wealthiest families have formal offices with full teams, every family can build an informal version.

Core Components of a Family Office

- **Chief Strategist:** You or your chosen successor
- **Tax advisors:** To minimize erosion
- **Insurance architects:** To leverage protective contracts
- **Investment managers:** To steward growth
- **Legal counsel:** To keep structures aligned with your wishes
- **Generational coaches:** To develop financial literacy and leadership

A family office creates continuity. Decisions are not made emotionally; they are made strategically.

The Legal Foundations of Lasting Wealth

To ensure your net worth lasts four to five generations, the legal structures must be airtight.

Key tools include:

- **Revocable Living Trusts:** For flexible asset control and probate avoidance.
- **Irrevocable Trusts:** For asset protection and long-term governance.

- **Foundations:** For charitable giving and tax advantages.
- **508(c)(1)(A) PMAs:** For mission-driven family initiatives.
- **Business Entities:** To hold real estate, equities, intellectual property, or family-owned companies.

The goal is simple: control everything, own nothing directly.

Culture: The True Glue of Generational Wealth

Wealth without culture is temporary. Culture without discipline is fragile.

Every lasting family builds a culture of:

- Ownership
- Education
- Accountability
- Celebration
- Stewardship
- Faith

This culture must be reinforced through:

- Family retreats
- Legacy dinners
- Annual giving traditions
- Storytelling and testimony nights
- Entrepreneurial training for youth
- Written family constitutions

Culture strengthens identity. Identity strengthens unity. And unity strengthens wealth.

Expanding the Formula: Beyond Net Worth

You've mastered the core formula: Assets – Liabilities = Net Worth.

Now expand it:

(Assets + Wisdom + Structure + Culture) – Liabilities = Generational Wealth

This formula captures the real components of a dynasty.

Assets alone can be lost.

Assets protected by wisdom, structure, and culture become unstoppable.

Your Role as the Legacy Architect

You are the one chosen to create the blueprint — the one called to break old cycles and build new systems.

Your mission now is to:

- Build the structure
- Teach the system
- Document the strategy
- Appoint and prepare successors
- Reinforce culture
- Prune liabilities
- Protect

CONCLUSION

Your Legacy Starts Now

Whether you are 18 or 88, the journey toward financial erudition begins the moment you decide to take ownership of your future. You now possess a blueprint — one rooted in history, strengthened by strategy, and refined for the realities of today's world.

This book was designed to shift your perspective from earning income to building systems. From understanding assets and liabilities, to mastering leverage and liquidity, to engineering generational structures, you have been introduced to the core principles that govern lasting wealth.

Wealth is not accidental. It is intentional.

For African American families in particular, this moment matters. Generations before us were denied access to information, tools, and opportunities that build legacy. That gap ends with knowledge — and knowledge must be applied. With modern strategies such as cash-value life insurance, trusts, private membership associations, real estate, and family governance systems, we now have the ability to reclaim, rebuild, and redirect our financial futures.

The responsibility now rests with you.

Re-read this book with your family. Discuss it at the dinner table. Turn concepts into conversations, and conversations into action. Create family goals. Write your family charter. Teach the next generation how assets work, how liquidity protects, and how leverage accelerates.

Do not wait for permission to build legacy. You are the permission.

When you commit to asset ownership, strategic protection, and intentional transfer, your net worth becomes more than a number — it becomes infrastructure. And when your infrastructure outlives you, your wealth becomes legacy.

You were chosen for this assignment.

Build boldly. Teach faithfully. Pass it forward.

Your legacy starts now.

Affirmation

I believe in NO DEBT and true wealth.

I believe in a stress-free lifestyle, paying limited taxes and minimal interest.

I believe in consuming as a real choice, not a compelled action.

I believe in generational intelligence and moving information forward to my network and family.

I believe in changing the paradigm of wealth-building for my family and for teaching others.

I believe in building great lives for future generations by creating new traditions and building legacies.

I believe in creating financial tools for my income while I am living and passing along those tools with wealth to the next three generations

Goals

Strategy

Assets

Net Worth

Notes

APPENDIX

Recommended Resources & Tools

The following resources support continued learning, implementation, and stewardship of the strategies outlined in this book:

Government & Regulatory Resources

- **IRS.gov** – Tax rules, retirement guidelines, and official tax publications
- **Social Security Administration** – Benefits eligibility, calculators, and planning tools
- **FDIC.gov** – Deposit insurance and consumer protection
- **SIPC.org** – Brokerage account protection

Education & Research

- **Investopedia.com** – Definitions, explanations, and financial education
- **NAIC.org (National Association of Insurance Commissioners)** – Insurance education and consumer guides

Business & Legal Infrastructure

- **Your State Secretary of State website** – Business and nonprofit filings
- **Local estate planning attorneys** – Trusts, wills, and succession planning
- **Licensed insurance professionals** – Policy design and risk strategy

ABOUT THE AUTHOR

Steven E. LaBroi

Steven E. LaBroi is a financial strategist, educator, and author committed to closing the wealth gap through education, asset-based planning, and generational strategy.

With over two decades of experience in financial services, Steven specializes in life insurance as an asset class, liquidity and leverage strategies, annuity and retirement planning, and multi-generational wealth architecture.

He is the **Chief Strategist of LaBroi Insurance Group LLC**, a nationwide independent life insurance and retirement strategy firm founded in 2015, and the **Executive Director of the nonprofit Millennial Banking Concept**, which equips young adults with financial literacy and wealth-building tools early in life.

Steven is the author of the Amazon bestseller Build Your Human Equity Line of Credit, a work that challenges traditional financial thinking and introduces life insurance as a powerful, cash–flow–driven asset.

His work focuses on helping families move from income dependence to asset ownership and from financial participation to financial control.

A graduate of Morehouse College with a degree in Finance and Banking, Steven brings a disciplined, culturally informed, and faith-centered approach to wealth building. His mission is simple yet profound: to help families establish financial systems that are strong enough to last four to five generations.

Steven lives by the belief that what you do with the money you earn matters more than how much you make—because legacy is built by structure, not salary.

Steven is also the director of Balance Life Health Wealth and Faith Institute, a ministry that assists individuals and families in balancing the base trilogy of human life: Health, Wealth, and Faith. Creating a nirvana state of mind when achieving balance with life's stress.

CONNECT WITH THE AUTHOR

Connect with the Author

The LaBroi Insurance Group
https://labroiinsurancegroup.com
slabroi@labroiinsurancegroup.com

Balance Life Health Wealth and Faith Institute
https://Blhwfinstitute.org
blhwfinstitutessm@protonmail.com

Part 1 by **Dr. Anita Johnson** is the foundation of this journey. It ntroduces the core ideas, guiding principles, and key reflections that shape everything that follows.

If these pages caused you to pause, question, or reconsider, that intention began in Part 1—where understanding is first formed and awareness takes root.

To fully appreciate the path forward, readers are encouraged to begin with Part 1 by Dr. Anita Johnson, where the journey starts and the groundwork is laid.

Made in the USA
Monee, IL
29 May 2026

50569014R00046